ALASKAN NATIVE CULTURES

VOLUME 1

TLINGIT

HAIDA

TSIMSHIAN

PAGES 2–3: This photograph of the Haida village of Howkan, taken in 1897, shows the influence of white culture in the shingled roofs and glass windows of the houses. The totem poles lining the beach, however, are enduring symbols of a traditional way of life.
(ALASKA STATE LIBRARY, WINTER & POND COLLECTION, PCA 87-050)

PAGE 3: Taking its English name from the raw material from which it was fashioned, a copper signified great wealth and prestige. Copper was obtained through trade with tribes in the interior and later from European explorers. The Europeans found that the sheet copper they used for repairing holes in the hulls of their ships was in great demand by the Native people. All coppers that have been analyzed to date were found to have been made of commercial metal.
(SEATTLE ART MUSEUM, CAT. NO. 91.1.55, PHOTO BY PAUL MACAPIA)

OPPOSITE: A crest hat is a clan's most prestigious ceremonial garment. Among the Tlingit, they are *at.óow*, an owned and valued thing. This carved wooden hat depicting a frog crest belongs to the Kiks.ádi clan of the Sitka Tlingit. Each of the spruce root basketry rings attached to the top of the hat represents a slave killed when the hat was dedicated.
(ALASKA STATE MUSEUM, JUNEAU, CAT. NO. II-B-1840)

PAGES 6–7: Contrary to popular belief, the Native people did not worship totem poles. The massive poles were carved with images of animals, ancestors, and supernatural beings representing family crests and history.
(PHOTO BY MARK KELLEY)

A portion of the proceeds from the sale of this book will be donated by the Alaska Natural History Association to the Sealaska Heritage Foundation's Scholarship/Heritage Study Program.

Editor: Angela Tripp
Art Director: Joanne Station
Writer: A.M. Kosh
Editorial Consultants: Margaret Seguin Anderson, Richard Dauenhauer, Nora Marks Dauenhauer, Marianne Boelscher Ignace
Editorial Assistants: Shira Gotshalk, Suzanne Rode

Albion Publishing Group
Santa Barbara, CA
(805) 963-6004
Lorie Bacon, Publisher

Published 1994. Printed in Hong Kong. ISBN 1-880352-34-6

ACKNOWLEDGMENTS

We would like to acknowledge and thank the following for their assistance and contribution to this book. The help of these individuals and groups has been invaluable: Frankie Barker, Diane Lin, and Debbe Smith, Alaska Natural History Association; Steve Henrikson, Alaska State Museum; Darlene Bezezekoff; Steve Brown; Janice Criswell; Scott Douglas; Jack Hudson; Richard Dauenhauer, Nora Marks Dauenhauer, Dennis Demmert, Donelle Everson, Lillian Sheakley, and Tim Wilson, Sealaska Heritage Foundation; Joni Packard, USDA Forest Service.

The following publishers have generously given permission to use extended quotations from copyrighted works: From *Haa Shuká, Our Ancestors: Tlingit Oral Narratives,* by Richard Dauenhauer and Nora Marks Dauenhauer. © 1987 by Sealaska Heritage Foundation. Published by Sealaska Heritage Foundation. Reprinted by permission. From *The Droning Shaman,* by Nora Marks Dauenhauer. © 1988 by Nora Marks Dauenhauer. Published by Black Current Press. Reprinted by permission. From *A Haida Potlatch,* by Ulli Steltzer. © 1984 by Ulli Steltzer. Published by Douglas & McIntyre. Reprinted by permission. From *The Raven Steals the Light,* by Bill Reid and Robert Bringhurst. © 1984 by Bill Reid and Robert Bringhurst. Published by University of Washington Press and Douglas & McIntyre. Reprinted by permission.

SOURCES CONSULTED

Emmons, George Thornton. *The Tlingit Indians.* Seattle: University of Washington Press, 1991.

Henrikson, Steve. "Yéil Koowú: The Reemergence of Ravenstail Weaving on the Northwest Coast." *American Indian Art Magazine* (Winter 1992): 58–67.

Holm, Bill. *Northwest Coast Indian Art: An Analysis of Form.* Seattle: University of Washington Press, 1965.

Holm, Bill. *The Box of Daylight: Northwest Coast Indian Art.* Seattle: Seattle Art Museum; Seattle: University of Washington Press, 1983.

Holm, Bill. *Spirit and Ancestor: A Century of Northwest Coast Indian Art at the Burke Museum.* Seattle: University of Washington Press, 1987.

Jonaitis, Aldona. *From the Land of the Totem Poles.* New York: American Museum of Natural History, 1988.

Jonaitis, Aldona. *Art of the Northern Tlingit.* Seattle: University of Washington Press, 1989.

Olson, Wallace M. *The Tlingit: An Introduction to their Culture and History.* 2d ed. Auke Bay, Alaska: Heritage Research, 1991.

Seguin, Margaret, ed. *The Tsimshian: Images of the Past: Views for the Present.* Vancouver: University of British Columbia Press, 1984.

Steltzer, Ulli. *A Haida Potlatch.* Seattle: University of Washington Press, 1984.

Sturtevant, William C., ed. *Handbook of North American Indians.* Vol. 7, *Northwest Coast.* Edited by Wayne Suttles. Washington: Smithsonian Institution, 1990.

CONTENTS

The northern Northwest Coast is a land of mist-shrouded islands and awe-inspiring glaciers. A land where ten-thousand-year-old spruce forests crowd miles of coastline and bald eagles fly overhead. A land that hosts the annual return of humpback whales to their summer feeding grounds. While most visitors know the coast of Southeast Alaska and British Columbia for the sights and sounds of its scenery and wildlife, many have yet to discover the cultural legacy of its oldest human inhabitants.

The abundance and beauty of the northern Northwest Coast is no secret to the Native people whose ancestors migrated here across the Bering Straits in prehistoric times. To the Tlingit, Haida, and Tsimshian people, the mainland and islands of the Alaskan panhandle and British Columbia have been home from time immemorial. The waterways of the Inside Passage where cruise ships now travel were once navigated by dugout canoes. The beaches and forests where campers pitch tents today were dotted with totem poles and cedar-plank houses not so long ago.

The Tlingit *(Klink-it),* Haida *(Hy-duh),* and Tsimshian *(Sim-see-on* or *Shim-shee-an)* had developed a rich and sophisticated culture long before the first white man set foot on these shores. They flourished in an environment that offered a vast and varied food supply and provided the raw material for clothing, shelter, and transportation. Despite the dissimilarity of their languages, the three cultures shared a remarkably similar way of life.

Traditional village life was destined to change forever with the arrival of European explorers in the late 1700s. By the turn of this century, many of the age-old customs were no longer observed. Within just the last twenty-five years, a resurgence of interest in their cultural heritage has led the Native people to rediscover the traditions of their ancestors. Through traditional song, dance, oratory, dramatic performance, and art, the Tlingit, Haida, and Tsimshian people have once again become a strong cultural presence on the northern Northwest Coast.

The perpetuation of traditional culture is due in large part to the dedication of the elders. By sharing their knowledge and skills, the elders have inspired the younger generations to take pride in their heritage and to keep the traditions alive. In a time when few people speak their Native language, it has become more important than ever to preserve the culture. The spirit among the Tlingit, Haida, and Tsimshian is one of hope for the future, and it is in the children that their greatest hope lies.

LEFT: At Celebration, many Native children take part in a traditional ceremony for the first time. Young people are included in the activities and, like their parents, wear clan regalia and participate in the dancing and singing. There has been a renewed effort in recent years to teach the children the value of ancient traditions.

(PHOTO BY MARK KELLEY)

ONE

TRADITIONAL CULTURE

People lived in Lituya Bay loooong ago.
Smoke houses and other houses were there.
There was a deserted place called Lituya Bay before
the white man migrated in from the sea.
At one point one morning a person went outside.
Then there was a white object that could be seen
way out on the sea bouncing on the waves.
At one point it was coming closer to the people.
"What's that? What's that, what's that?"
"It's something different!"
"It's something different!"
"Is it Raven?"
"Maybe that's what it is."
"I think that's what it is—
Raven who created the world.
He said he would come back again."

—from The Coming of the First White Man,
a Tlingit narrative told by George R. Betts
Tlingit, Eagle, Kaagwaantaan Clan
From Haa Shuká, Our Ancestors: Tlingit Oral Narratives
by Richard Dauenhauer and Nora Marks Dauenhauer

ABOVE: Masks played an important role in Native rituals. Masks and other wood carvings were used ceremonially to mark important times of change in a person's life, including puberty, marriage, and death.
(SHELDON JACKSON MUSEUM, CAT. NO. I-A-142)

PAGES 10–11: A Tlingit village in Juneau became home to the many Natives who joined in the gold rush activities of the late 1800s. This photo, taken in 1910, reveals only some of the influences of white culture on Native life.
(ALASKA STATE LIBRARY, WINTER & POND COLLECTION, PCA 87-1328)

A CHANGING CULTURE

With the coming of the first white man in 1741, life for the Tlingit, Haida, and Tsimshian people changed forever. As the eighteenth century drew to a close, European and American explorers and traders were no longer an uncommon sight on the northern Northwest Coast. The Native people were shrewd and respected traders and for the most part benefited from trade relations. But both the whites and the Native people wanted control of the fur trade, which resulted in skirmishes and led to all-out war between the Russians and the Tlingits at the Battles of Sitka in 1802 and 1804.

With the whites also came disease, which had a more profound and far-reaching impact on the Native population than did any battle. Entire villages were decimated by epidemics of smallpox and other diseases for which the Native people had no natural immunity. Villages that had been occupied for thousands of years were left abandoned and the few people who did survive often moved away to live with distant family members.

Further change came with the arrival of the missionaries. The effect of their presence on the lives of the Native people cannot be easily defined. Many worked to improve conditions in the villages and encouraged cultural expression. Others pressured the Native people to adopt Christianity at the expense of their own language and customs.

Despite discouragement by missionaries, a few Native artisans continued to produce traditional art, finding a flourishing market among collectors and tourists. By the late nineteenth and early twentieth centuries, the growing collection of Native artifacts in the museums of the world had sparked new interest in northern Northwest Coast cultures.

But as the world was gaining a greater appreciation for traditional Native culture, that culture was changing very rapidly. The transition to a different way of life coincided with the advent of photography, and it was through this new medium that the extent of change was conveyed. Historical photographs are a strong visual testament to the fortitude of the Native people who, despite foreign influence and the adoption of many Western customs, did not reject their heritage.

RIGHT: In 1887, under the leadership of missionary William Duncan, a group of Tsimshian relocated from their original settlement at Metlakatla on the coast of British Columbia to New Metlakatla in Alaska to establish a community based on utopian and communalistic ideals. The journey to this previously uninhabited site was made by canoe, which was the main mode of travel for all the coastal Native groups.

(ALASKA STATE LIBRARY, DUNCAN COLLECTION, PCA 43-65)

BELOW: Juneau photographers Winter and Pond documented Native life at a time when change was extreme. This studio portrait, taken in the early 1900s, shows Native children dressed in Western-style clothing—a cultural feature accepted earlier by the Native people.

(ALASKA STATE LIBRARY, WINTER & POND COLLECTION, PCA 87-071)

INUPIAQ ESKIMO

BERING SEA

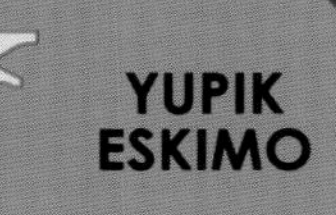

ALEUT

Kodiak Island

PACIFIC ESKIMO

Aleutian Islands

NATIVE CULTURES

ALASKA & THE NORTHWEST COAST

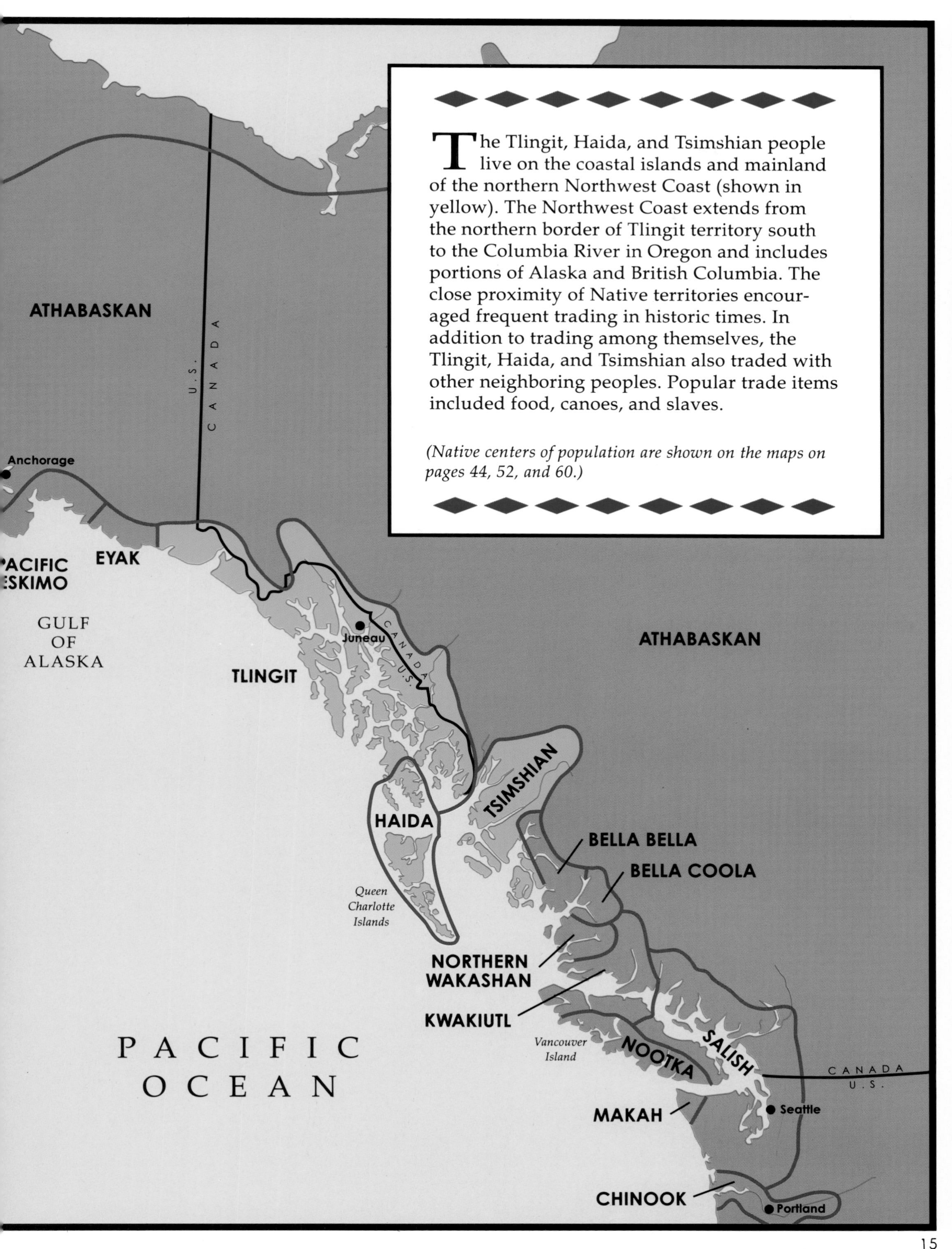

The Tlingit, Haida, and Tsimshian people live on the coastal islands and mainland of the northern Northwest Coast (shown in yellow). The Northwest Coast extends from the northern border of Tlingit territory south to the Columbia River in Oregon and includes portions of Alaska and British Columbia. The close proximity of Native territories encouraged frequent trading in historic times. In addition to trading among themselves, the Tlingit, Haida, and Tsimshian also traded with other neighboring peoples. Popular trade items included food, canoes, and slaves.

(Native centers of population are shown on the maps on pages 44, 52, and 60.)

SOCIAL ORGANIZATION

Tlingit and Haida society is organized into moieties, or two separate but complementary groups. Every person is born into one of two groups called Raven and Eagle (also called Crow and Wolf). Each moiety consists of many clans, which forms the basis for political organization. The clans are further divided into house groups, or lineages. A person's loyalty belongs first and foremost to the house group.

Prior to European contact, the Tsimshian probably also had a dual societal structure at the village level, but it was replaced in some areas by a four-group system in which the groups were called phratries. Although they had different names, the moieties of the Tlingit, Haida, and Tsimshian were aligned so that marriages could be made and trade relationships established among the tribes.

Marriages were arranged and social obligations met according to moiety. A person always married into the opposite moiety. Today, although many Native people recognize their moiety affiliation, marriage to one of the same moiety or to a non-Native is neither uncommon nor forbidden as it once was. However, as in historic times, it is still common practice to provide emotional and monetary support to members of the opposite moiety in times of loss or celebration.

Native society is matrilineal. That is, a person's familial relationships are traced through the mother's line. For example, the children of a Raven mother and Eagle father are Ravens like their mother, and traditionally they inherited property from their mother's brother rather than from their father, who was of the opposite moiety. Boys were raised primarily by their maternal uncles and girls by their mothers and maternal aunts.

A strict ranking system governed social organization. The nobility consisted of leaders, or chiefs, and their relatives, followed by the lower-ranking commoners. The lowliest class was comprised of slaves, who had no rights and were excluded from

ABOVE: A Nisga'a (Tsimshianic-speaking) family posing in ceremonial regalia. Although most chiefs were men, the woman (third from left) is dressed in a ravenstail robe, which indicates that she most likely held a position of leadership in her clan. This is the only known historical photograph of a ravenstail robe in ceremonial use. (CANADIAN MUSEUM OF CIVILIZATION, OTTAWA, ONTARIO, NEG. NO. 70685)

the social system. The Tsimshian recognized a fourth class of people who were free but who had no rights in a house group.

Each clan had a hereditary leader, who oversaw his clan's property and resources and decided how they would be used. Each house group within a clan was presided over by a house leader or house spokesperson who was most often, but not always, male. The leader of the house group that owned the village site was the highest ranking of the leaders.

SUBSISTENCE

Although techniques have changed, subsistence is still important in Native life today. Many families return to traditional hunting and fishing lands every year. Technology has made some of the work easier, but the types of food eaten and the method of preparation have remained the same.

The Native people had access to a great variety and abundance of food sources. Their subsistence activities were determined by the seasonal cycle and availability of local species. For example, in Tlingit territory, early spring was the time to catch halibut, while further south, the Haida of Graham Island hunted birds and bird eggs.

Tribal clans moved from their permanent winter homes to traditional fishing and hunting camps for the summer. Fish and shellfish were the mainstay of the Native diet, followed in importance by sea mammals, vegetation, and land mammals.

Fish were caught with a hook and line, by spearing, and with nets and fish weirs, or traps. The people caught halibut, eulachon, five species of salmon, herring, trout, cod, and rock cod. Herring eggs and the roe of pink and chum salmon were a delicacy. Shellfish such as clams and scallops were considered "common" food because they were abundant and available year round.

Men did all the hunting, including that of sea mammals. They hunted from canoes and used harpoons to kill harbor seal, fur seal, sea lions, porpoise, and sea otter. Women harvested and preserved berries, including salmonberries, soapberries, and high bush cranberries, and gathered other edible vegetation. Seaweed was a favorite food, especially when prepared with herring eggs.

Little hunting was done in the winter, since it was usually possible to gather enough food in the summer to sustain an entire house group through winter. Meat from seal, deer, mountain goats, Dall sheep, bears, and salmon was preserved through drying or smoking. Meat and fish eggs were also preserved by being stored in oil rendered from the eulachon fish, herring, salmon heads, seal blubber, and mountain goat fat. Although the Native people did not hunt whales, they did use whale meat and blubber when the animals washed ashore.

BELOW: Intricately carved bowls, like this Tlingit piece, were used to hold eulachon oil, a delicacy derived from the eulachon fish and served with dried salmon and a variety of other foods. The oil was a main source of dietary fat for the Native people and was a highly valued trade item. The majority of eulachon oil came from Tsimshian territory, where the eulachon fish flourished at the mouth of the Nass River.
(SHELDON JACKSON MUSEUM, CAT. NO. I-A-269)

RIGHT: This collection of halibut gear includes hooks, floats, and line. Designed to catch fish up to several hundred pounds, the halibut hooks were carved with figures thought to have the power to lure this spring-harvested staple.

(ALASKA STATE LIBRARY, MERRILL COLLECTION, PCA 57-106)

BELOW: Temporary fishing camps served as the base for summer subsistence activities. By 1895, when this photograph was taken, store-bought goods such as iron pots were used in addition to traditional implements like the ladle made of mountain sheep horn, shown lying on a piece of driftwood in the foreground.

(ALASKA STATE LIBRARY, WINTER & POND COLLECTION, PCA 87-079)

ABOVE: The "Monster House" of Chief Weah in Masset was one of the largest Haida houses ever built. Measuring fifty-four by fifty-five feet, the structure contained a bilevel central fire pit and enough living space for more than fifty people.

(AMERICAN MUSEUM OF NATURAL HISTORY, DEPARTMENT OF LIBRARY SERVICES, NEG. NO. 24482)

LEFT: Large wooden screens were used by house leaders to partition off their living quarters from communal areas. The screens were carved and painted with a clan's crest figures.
(SHELDON JACKSON MUSEUM, CAT. NO. I-A-222)

PAGES 22–23: Tlingit men and boys display crest objects inside the Whale House in Klukwan. The magnificent house screen and house posts are known to be some of the most remarkable examples of Northwest Coast art. The long wood worm feast dish on the top tier and the massive "Mother Basket" in the foreground were both used during ceremonies to serve guests enormous amounts of food.
(ALASKA STATE LIBRARY, WINTER & POND COLLECTION, PCA 87-010)

SHELTER

The Northwest Coast is covered with a dense rain forest of cedar, spruce, and hemlock that crowds up against narrow expanses of rocky beaches. Cedar and spruce trees provided the Tlingit, Haida, and Tsimshian the raw material with which to build enormous houses for the members of their extended families.

The rectangular-shaped houses made by the three groups were very similar in construction and shared many of the same features. While the Tlingit lived in houses made of spruce or cedar planks, the Haida and Tsimshian built theirs solely of red cedar. In coastal villages, the houses were placed closely together in a row on the beach, with the entrance facing the shore. Four main house posts supported the roofs, and the wall planks were fitted into the corner or midwall posts. The house posts were carved and painted with totemic and ancestral figures.

An oval hole just tall enough to allow an adult to enter served as the main entrance. The Haida and Tsimshian sometimes placed carved totem poles flush against their house facades, and it was through an oval hole in these totem poles that people entered the house. The structures often accommodated fifty people or more.

The main living space was an excavated pit that measured approximately five feet deep and thirty feet square and was usually lined with cedar plank retaining walls. Some Haida houses had a central area, or pit, that was excavated into tiers. Each house was warmed by a central fire that also served as a cooking area. The smoke was vented through a smoke hole in the roof.

TRADE & WARFARE

Contact among the Tlingit, Haida, and Tsimshian was frequent because of the extensive trade network they maintained. By the late 1700s, when the first European explorers and traders arrived on the Northwest Coast, trade routes and relationships were well established among the Native people.

Food, canoes, and slaves were the primary trade goods. Those items a clan was unable to secure for itself were often obtained through trade with neighboring clans or other tribes. Occasionally, leaders from different tribes formed formal trading relationships based on corresponding moieties or phratries.

One of the most valuable trade items was the eulachon fish, whose oil, or "grease," was considered a delicacy. Some Tlingit had access to eulachon streams, but most, like the Haida, were dependent upon trade with the Tsimshian to obtain large amounts of eulachon.

Trade sometimes led to warfare as a result of groups wanting to establish or maintain control of key trade routes and resources. War was also waged for revenge, plunder, and to capture slaves. The Haida, especially, were notorious for their propensity to war. Attacks on the enemy were most often made at night to gain the advantage of surprise. Men were slain, and their heads and scalps kept as trophies. Women and children were usually taken as slaves.

ABOVE: Along with head and neck protection, a Tlingit warrior wore a tunic made from untanned moose hide obtained in trade with tribes from the interior. A suit of wood-slat armor was typically worn over the tunic, covering the body from neck to knee. With the introduction of firearms, wooden armor became obsolete. Weapons included spears, daggers, war clubs, and bows and arrows.

(ALASKA STATE LIBRARY, MERRILL COLLECTION, PCA 57-113)

RIGHT: This war helmet belonged to Katlean, a Kiks.ádi Tlingit war leader who fought against the Russians in the battle of Sitka in 1804. The wooden helmet is carved to represent a raven and is covered with bear skin and fur. The eyes are inlaid with copper. War helmets were intentionally designed to convey a fearsome appearance so as to gain psychological advantage over the enemy.

(SHELDON JACKSON MUSEUM, CAT. NO. I.A.131)

RIGHT: Bentwood boxes were constructed from spruce, yew, and red or yellow cedar. A wooden plank was first heated to make it pliable and then bent at right angles to form a rectangular shape. The two ends were joined with pegs or with laces pulled through drilled holes. A fitted lid and bottom completed the watertight boxes, which were put to a variety of uses, including the transporting and storing of food and ceremonial regalia.

(ROYAL BRITISH COLUMBIA MUSEUM, CAT. NO. 1635)

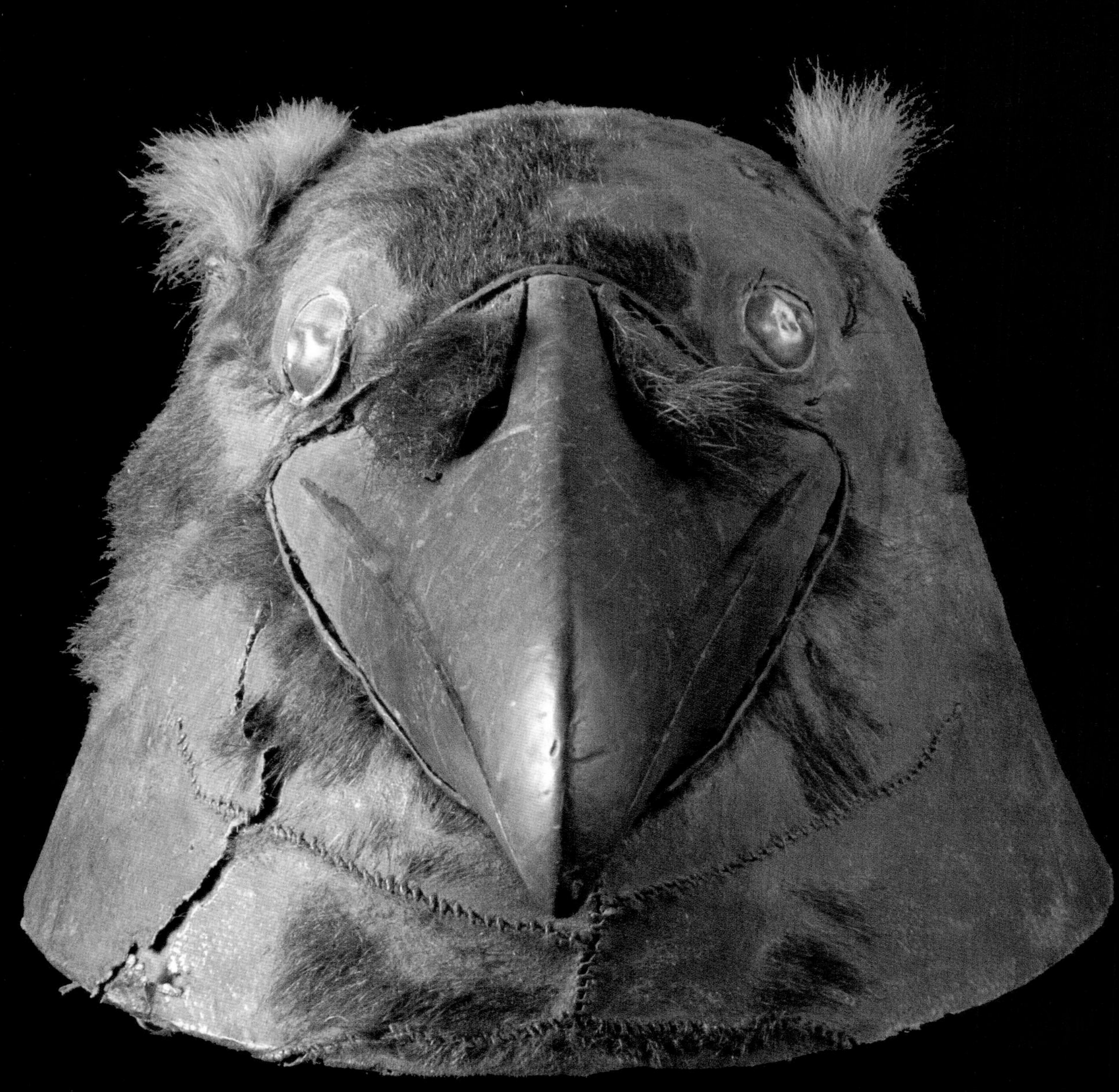

TRANSPORTATION

Canoes were the primary mode of transportation in an environment dominated by waterways. The larger seaworthy canoes were used to transport goods and people the length of the Northwest Coast. Although the Tlingit, Haida, and Tsimshian all were skilled in canoe making, the Haida made the best canoes.

Haida canoes were made of western red cedar that grew abundantly on the Queen Charlotte Islands. A finished canoe, hewn from a single tree, often spanned sixty feet from prow to stern and could carry six to eight tons of cargo. The vessels were built to withstand the open seas and had two masts and sails for use on long voyages. The large size and fine workmanship of Haida canoes made them highly valued trade items.

Tlingit canoes, although much smaller than the enormous Haida canoes, were also uniquely constructed to suit a specific purpose. The Yakutat Tlingit in the north made heavy-prowed canoes for seal hunting in ice-choked water, while the Chilkat and Dry Bay Tlingit preferred shallow draft canoes of cottonwood designed for navigating rivers.

Although there were few destinations that could not be reached by canoe, the Tsimshian and mainland Tlingit occasionally found it necessary to use snowshoes in winter for walking overland. Snowshoes were obtained in trade from the Eyak and Athabaskan tribes to the north. Hand-drawn sleds were also commonly used for travel among some of the northernmost Tlingit clans, as well as among some Tsimshian.

RIGHT: The Haida were renowned on the Northwest Coast for the superior craftsmanship of their canoes. This nineteenth-century model accurately represents the sculptural form of a large Haida canoe. The painted black hull and elaborately detailed ends are typical of the decoration seen on many of the large northern canoes. The design on this model is thought to have been painted by noted Haida artist Charles Edenshaw. *(THOMAS BURKE MEMORIAL WASHINGTON STATE MUSEUM, CAT. NO. 1-3004, PHOTO BY EDUARDO CALDERON)*

ABOVE: In 1890, when this photo was taken, canoe building was becoming obsolete with the use of commercially designed vessels and, by 1910, gas-powered boats. These Tsimshian, however, still practice the rigorous tradition of hollowing and shaping a cedar log with adzes.

(ALASKA STATE LIBRARY, DUNCAN COLLECTION, PCA 43-6)

CEREMONIES

Ceremonialism has always been an integral part of Native culture because it provides a forum for maintaining social order and serves as a vital component of the grieving process after the loss of a loved one. Through ritual feasts and potlatches, rank and kinship are reinforced on all levels—between individuals, moieties, and tribes.

Ceremonies include potlatches and feasts, which are hosted by high-ranking members of a clan. Potlatches are elaborate ceremonies held to memorialize the deceased or to acknowledge both the completion of a new house and its spokesman's new position as house leader. While potlatches usually include feasting, feasts are held separately to mark important occasions such as the first naming of a child, marriage, death, and for honoring high-ranking visitors or to enhance one's own prestige.

At potlatches, property is ceremonially distributed by the hosts to the guests. The guests are usually members of the opposite moiety, and receive gifts as payment for their services. Traditionally, when a person died, relatives of the opposite moiety bathed and dressed the body in preparation for its lying in state and subsequent cremation. Later, the deceased person's clans people held a memorial potlatch that not only served to mark the deceased's passage and acknowledge the heir, but also to pay relatives for their services and support in a time of grief. Such memorials are still common in Native communities.

BELOW: Song, dance, and oral narrative are all integral to Native ceremony. Rhythm instruments, such as drums, rattles, and dance aprons decorated with bird beaks and deer or elk hooves, are used for accompaniment. Because of the similarities of design among the Tlingit, Haida, and Tsimshian, it has been impossible to determine from which of the three cultures this particular hide drum originated.
(THOMAS BURKE MEMORIAL WASHINGTON STATE MUSEUM, CAT. NO. 1-978)

RIGHT: In 1904, the Sitka Tlingit and their Yakutat Tlingit guests gathered for a potlatch, although potlatches were officially discouraged at the time. This photograph shows the variety of ceremonial regalia worn at potlatches. The women in the front row wear imitations of a Russian sailor's hat.
(ALASKA STATE LIBRARY, MERRILL COLLECTION, PCA 57-21)

LEFT: Dancing headdresses were some of the most elaborately decorated ceremonial objects, and were worn by leaders and dancers at potlatches. This Tlingit headdress is made of wood, sea lion whiskers, abalone shell, ermine skins, and the tail feathers and iridescent, green head feathers of a mallard duck. Loose white eagle down—a symbol of peace and welcome to guests at a potlatch—fills the crown to waft down over those in attendance when the dancing begins.

(ALASKA STATE MUSEUM, JUNEAU, CAT. NO. II-B-1018)

ABOVE: Although Chilkat dancing robes are named after the Chilkat tribe of Tlingit who specialized in their weaving, they are Tsimshian in origin. The robes are a ceremonial garment worn at potlatches. Classic Chilkat robes are highly prized and demonstrate an abstractness in design rarely seen in other northern Northwest Coast art. The technique is so difficult because unlike most weaving that produces geometric patterns, Chilkat weaving allows for curvilinear and circular shapes to be woven. This nineteenth-century robe depicts a diving whale.

(ROYAL BRITISH COLUMBIA MUSEUM, CAT. NO. 9535)

PAGES 32–33: Attendance as guests at a potlatch held with it the responsibility to bear witness to social and political events. These dancers bank their canoes on the shores of the Chilkat River during their arrival at a potlatch held in the late 1800s.

(ALASKA STATE LIBRARY, WINTER & POND COLLECTION, PCA 87-043)

462
Wrangell Medicine Man.
W.P.Co
Juneau.

SPIRITUAL LIFE

The Native people's respect for the natural environment was reflective of their relationship to the spiritual world. They believed that all matter—including animals and natural features such as glaciers and mountains—possessed a soul.

Spirits had the power to cause disaster and to bring good luck. To avoid bringing harm to themselves or their loved ones by incurring the wrath of an angry spirit, people treated all living things with reverence. Both animals and humans were eventually reincarnated when they died.

Although a distinction was made between the physical and spiritual worlds, the boundary was permeable. Spirits affected the everyday lives of people and were often blamed as the cause of illness and bad luck. Misfortune was attributed to the failure to acknowledge and address the spirits with respect.

Communication with the spirit world was the province of the shamans. Shamans were the most powerful members of their clans. The Native people believed that shamans could cure sickness caused by the influence of spirits and witches, foretell the future, control the weather, and bring success in hunting and war.

Today, Native people are members of various Christian churches, but many people retain and practice traditional respect for animals and the environment. Shamanism is no longer practiced.

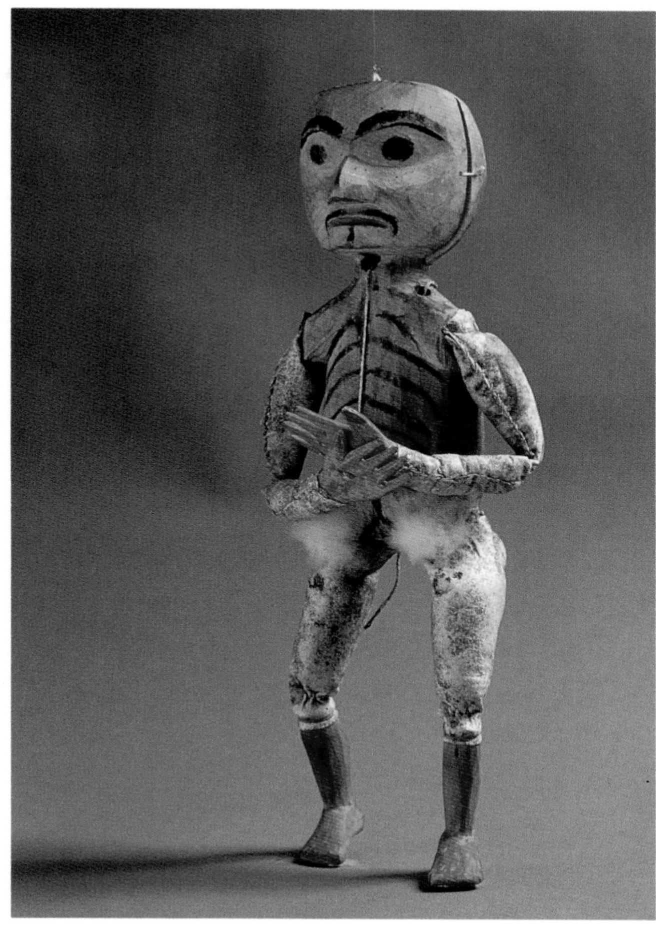

ABOVE: Marionettes, masks, and other illusory devices were used by shamans to convey supernatural powers. This Tsimshian marionette is made of wood and animal skin. The puppet's hands were manipulated with a cord threaded through the neck. The head is hollow and doubles as a rattle.
(THOMAS BURKE MEMORIAL WASHINGTON STATE MUSEUM, CAT. NO. 1-1653, PHOTO BY EDUARDO CALDERON)

LEFT: Rattles had a variety of uses but always implied the presence of supernatural power. Shamans used rattles in curing the sick and for calling for assistance from the spirit world. Raven rattles like the one pictured at left were used by chiefs in ceremonial dances.
(SEATTLE ART MUSEUM, CAT. NO. 91.1.57, PHOTO BY PAUL MACAPIA)

LEFT: This Tlingit shaman was a spiritual leader who controlled the spirits of humans and animals. He used his power to cure the sick and foresee the future. His ungroomed appearance was a sign of his status—it was believed that if a shaman cut or combed his hair, he would lose his power to communicate with the spirits.
(ALASKA STATE LIBRARY, WINTER & POND COLLECTION, PCA 87-250)

ART

Native art of the northern Northwest Coast is characterized by a highly stylized and refined design. The recurrent use of animal imagery reflects the importance of the natural world in the everyday life of the people. Clans identify with specific animals, called crests, and claim the exclusive right to their representation. Crests are used to identify clans and are displayed on totem poles, house posts, ceremonial clothing, canoes, grave markers, and on any object that necessitates a mark of clan ownership.

Art traditionally decorated everything from the most utilitarian of objects to the grandest of totem poles. Ceremonial art such as masks, headdresses, and rattles played—and still play—an integral part in the oral tradition. Since there was no written language until modern times, ceremonial art was used symbolically to visually enhance the singing, dancing, and storytelling.

The availability of trees as a raw material makes wood the most common medium for artistic expression. Carved designs are created with a conventionalized set of shapes. The primary element, called a formline, defines the outline of the image in black. The secondary elements are shown in red and the tertiary areas in blue-green.

It is difficult to differentiate the two-dimensional art, such as carved and painted house screens, of the Tlingit, Haida, and Tsimshian. However, in three-dimensional works like headdresses, masks, and totem poles, the stylistic differences among the three are evident. For example, on Tlingit artifacts, there is a deeper cut between the orb of the eye and the eyebrow.

Carving and engraving were traditionally done by men, while women wove the intricate and highly prized Chilkat and ravenstail robes. The women also wove spruce root hats and baskets and mastered the technique of appliquéing robes made from trade cloth. All Northwest Coast Native art, regardless of the medium, is distinguished by balance and proportion.

Despite a rigid artistic tradition, originality flourished. The introduction through trade of new materials such as sheet copper, metal coins, and flannel blankets challenged long-established artistic principles. The artists' ability to adapt traditional designs to new media was a testament to their consummate skill.

ABOVE: Chilkat robes were woven by women, based on designs created by men who painted them on wooden pattern boards. The Chilkat weaving technique was very complex and a single robe could take more than a year to complete.
(ALASKA STATE LIBRARY, WINTER & POND COLLECTION, PCA 87-197)

OPPOSITE: Since many early explorers did not describe seeing totem poles, it is possible that totem poles, like this Wrangell pole that belonged to Kahl-Teen, a Tlingit leader, flourished with the introduction of metal woodworking tools. But some of the best carvings in existence today were made with stone tools.
(ALASKA STATE LIBRARY, WINTER & POND COLLECTION, PCA 87-128)

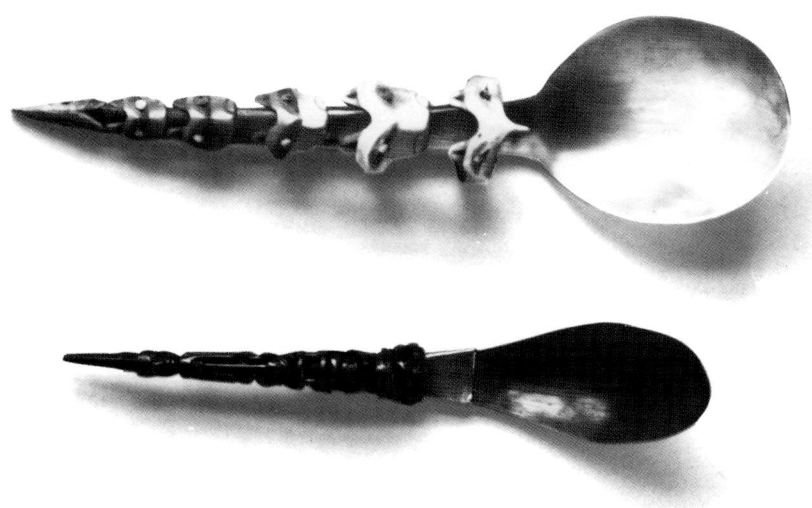

LEFT: These spoons were cut from cow (top) and mountain goat (bottom) horn and steam-molded into a rounded shape. Despite their utilitarian function, many spoons were ornately carved with the same complex and detailed crest figures found on ceremonial objects.
(ALASKA STATE LIBRARY, WINTER & POND COLLECTION, PCA 87-171)

LEFT: The eagle headdress by contemporary Tlingit artist Nathan Jackson exemplifies a mastery of age-old artistic forms. The work is based on a headdress collected by Russian explorers in the early 1800s.

(ALASKA STATE MUSEUM, JUNEAU, CAT. NO. II-B-1846)

BELOW: Argillite is a rare black shale found in the rugged mountains of the Queen Charlotte Islands. The Haida quarried the soft stone and carved it into complex and finely detailed curios. Although a few items were created for Native use, argillite pieces, such as this chest decorated with highly defined sculptural figures, were primarily sold or traded to non-Natives in their quest for souvenirs.

(ROYAL BRITISH COLUMBIA MUSEUM, CAT. NO. 13528)

ABOVE: With the introduction of trade cloth, the Native people incorporated new materials into the making of traditional clothing. The sleeves, yoke, and hem of this Yakutat Tlingit deer skin shirt are made of red wool trimmed with black cotton.

(ALASKA STATE MUSEUM, JUNEAU, CAT. NO. II-B-1376)

RIGHT: For all their functionality, spruce root baskets were beautifully made. Tlingit and Haida baskets were made of split spruce root and woven with a two-strand twining technique. Tlingit basket makers often incorporated false embroidery in their designs. Bleached or dyed grass stems were wrapped around spruce root strands, creating multicolored geometric designs. An example of false embroidery is seen in the basket on the right. This basket displays both traditional geometric patterns as well as naturalistic salmon and eye designs. The use of easily identifiable images was a later development designed to appeal to the non-Native tourist market.

(ALASKA STATE MUSEUM, JUNEAU, CAT. NO. II-B-1700)

Beauty was in everything in the lives of our ancestors. Everything they used in their daily lives—their bowls, their boxes, their robes—everything was decorated and made beautiful. Our people surrounded themselves with beauty, and it all meant something. It told something about you.

Janice Criswell, Artist
Haida / Tlingit
Raven
Owl Clan

RIGHT: The spruce root hat's tight weave and conical shape helped protect the Native people from the constant rain. Split-object designs were painted on or woven into the hat. The workmanship of some hats was so fine that they were elevated beyond pure function to become ceremonial objects.
(ROYAL BRITISH COLUMBIA MUSEUM, CAT. NO. 7954)

LEFT: Among the Tsimshianic-speaking groups, initiates of secret societies often wore elaborate masks like this nineteenth-century piece depicting a long-beaked crane. The mask is decorated with carved wooden skulls and shredded cedar bark for feathers. Adopted from the Bella Bella, secret society performances were dramatizations of supernatural powers and existed alongside the Tsimshianic masking tradition known as the *halait*. (AMERICAN MUSEUM OF NATURAL HISTORY, DEPARTMENT OF LIBRARY SERVICES, NEG. NO. K16481)

TWO

DÉIX̲

THE TLINGIT

Among your silent faces
I still hear
your song,
in many different voices,
grandfathers of mine.

— *Nora Marks Dauenhauer*
Tlingit
Raven
Lukaax̲.ádi Clan
From The Droning Shaman,
poems by Nora Marks Dauenhauer

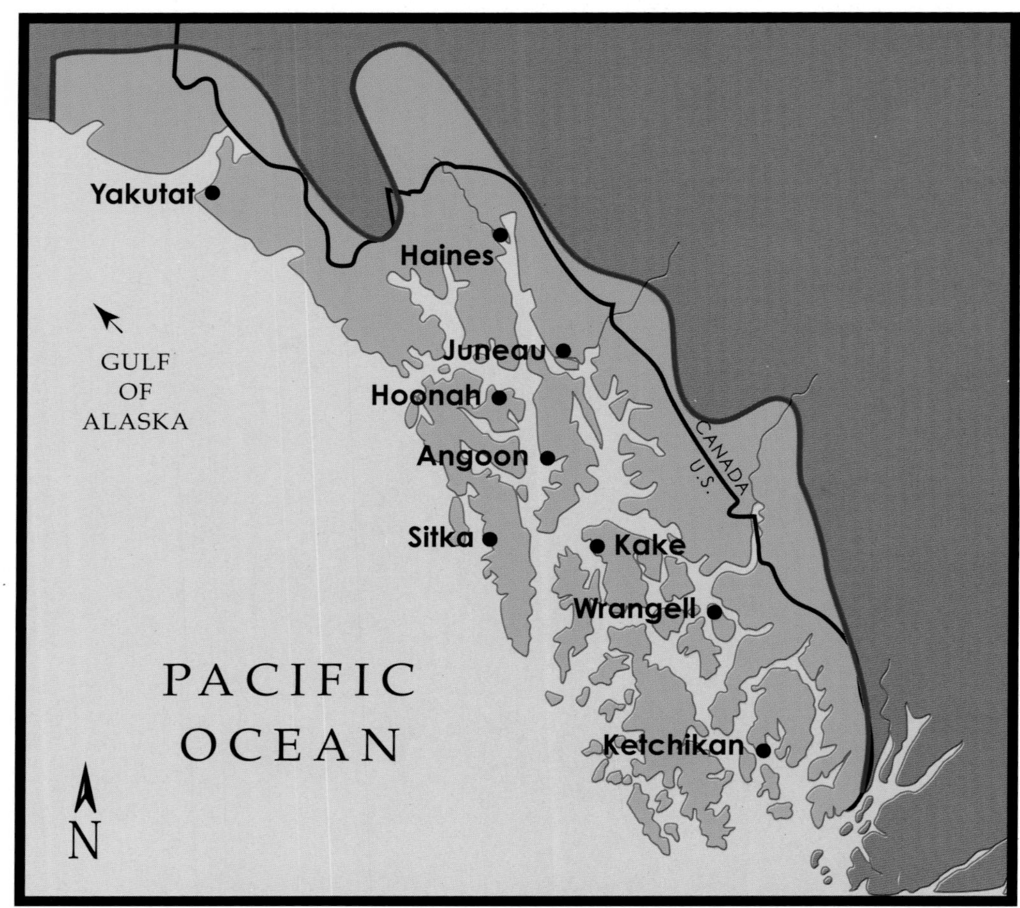

LEFT: Tlingit territory historically encompassed the islands, coast, and inland area of Southeast Alaska. Many of today's modern cities such as Juneau and Sitka were built on traditional village sites and continue to be home to many Tlingit.

(See Map on pages 14–15 for an expanded view of Alaska and the Northwest Coast.)

OPPOSITE: The wearing of crest hats and clothing is a way to show pride in one's heritage and to recognize family and clan affiliations.
(PHOTO BY MARK KELLEY)

PAGES 42–43: Traditional songs and dances are being kept alive by the elders. The Mt. Fairweather Dancers from Hoonah are just one of the many dance groups that are taking part in a cultural revival.
(PHOTO BY MARK KELLEY)

A CELEBRATION OF HERITAGE

The Tlingit people of Southeast Alaska have occupied their ancestral homeland for thousands of years. Historic Tlingit tribal land encompasses the coastal area that stretches 500 miles from Yakutat north of Glacier Bay south to Ketchikan. Its eastern border extends inland to southern Yukon and northern British Columbia, Canada. Today, many Native people retain rights to the land and subsist on its wealth of natural resources, just as their ancestors did before them.

In this rugged land of sea, rivers, islands, forests, and towering mountains, the Tlingit have built a rich culture that has persevered in the face of oppression and discrimination. Despite outside influence on Tlingit culture, which began with the arrival of Russian explorers in the late 1700s and has continued into this century, ancient traditions have been preserved by the elders and passed from generation to generation.

That Tlingit culture has withstood the passage of time is a testament to its ageless value. Assimilation has not extinguished the practice of ancient traditions, but rather has enabled the Tlingit people to determine their place in today's world. Contemporary culture has evolved into a mixture of the old and new. The modern Tlingit is a student, a dentist, a disc jockey, a lawyer, a small business owner—all are Alaskans, all are Americans, but being Tlingit is the most unifying commonality because it reflects a shared heritage.

The Sealaska Heritage Foundation, located in Juneau, is dedicated to preserving, promoting, and maintaining the cultures and heritage of the Tlingit, Haida, and Tsimshian people. It serves the general public as well as the Native community by producing educational materials and providing programs that directly benefit the Native people. Included among its many programs are the Language and Cultural Studies Program, which is working to publish a series of titles on the stories, history, and traditions of Southeast Alaska's Native people, as well as a scholarship program that provides financial support for those seeking a college education or an apprenticeship with a Native artist.

An integral part of Tlingit culture is its rich artistic heritage. Among the most powerful of its art forms is dramatic performance, which is rooted in the ancient traditions of oral literature, dance, and song. The oral tradition is being kept alive through the Naa Kahidi Theater's dramatic presentations of traditional legends. The theater was established in 1986 by the Sealaska Heritage Foundation and has since traveled widely throughout the United States and Europe. The Naa Kahidi (Tlingit for "clan house") Theater uses replicas of traditional regalia and props to enact compelling dramas about the history, myths, and customs of the Native people.

Dramatic performances and oratory provide a means by which to inspire young people to take an active role in their cultural traditions. Since the

RIGHT: This sea lion war helmet by Steve Brown is a contemporary re-creation of a Tlingit artifact. The carving is a fine example of the way in which traditional artists adapt formline design to a three-dimensional surface. (ALASKA STATE MUSEUM, JUNEAU, CAT. NO. I-B-130)

BELOW: Drum making is just one of the many activities in which children can participate at the annual culture camps. The camps are attended by both Native and non-Native children and are conducted under the guidance of tribal elders. (COURTESY CHILKOOT CULTURE CAMP)

traditions are often unknown to the younger generations, the annual culture camps held in Kake and Haines provide an opportunity for young people, Native and non-Native alike, to be exposed to traditional values and to learn the old customs. They are taught by the elders, who instruct them in such activities as bead work, wood carving, drum making, dancing, and storytelling, and who teach them subsistence methods and traditional ways for preparing food.

The Chilkoot Culture Camp was founded in Haines by the late Austin Hammond of the Lukaax̱.ádi clan. He was a well-known and respected Tlingit elder and leader whose mission was to preserve the cultural traditions of his people. For the younger generation, elders are their link with the past. The elders are valued for their knowledge and respected for their contribution to keeping the ancient traditions alive.

The importance of perpetuating traditions through use and practice was the impetus behind the Sealaska Heritage Foundation's sponsoring of a biennial gathering to celebrate the Tlingit, Haida, and Tsimshian cultures. The three-day event gives clan groups, families, and individuals the opportunity to actively participate in a contemporary ceremonial designed to help foster and revive knowledge of old traditions. Celebration offers a contemporary, secular context for performance of traditional song and dance. It is also a time to conduct the more somber business of formalizing adoptions and giving Tlingit names to the children.

ABOVE: Tlingit carver Nathan Jackson of Ketchikan is a highly regarded Native artist. His body of work includes pieces that range in size from life-size masks to enormous totem poles, one of which is shown here in an early stage of creation.
(PHOTO BY MARK KELLEY)

Celebration is an occasion for recognizing the importance of one's relatives by publicly acknowledging their support. Such recognition serves to reaffirm the individual's place in society and emphasizes the ancient values of respect and reciprocity that illustrate the rich legacy of Tlingit culture.

The Box of Daylight

Raven, the Trickster, was walking along the beach. It was the beginning of time. The world was dark. The sun, moon, and stars were kept in boxes by a wealthy old man who lived with his beautiful daughter at the Headwaters of the Nass River. The Fishermen of the Night told Raven about the treasures, and he hurried to the house of Nass Shaak Aan<u>k</u>aawu.

Raven transformed his spirit into a tiny spruce needle, which the young woman swallowed when she drank. She became pregnant and gave birth to Raven in the form of a human child.

Like all grandfathers, old Nass Shaak Aan<u>k</u>aawu loved his little grandson, and he gave him anything he asked for to play with. So when the child asked to play with the stars, moon, and sun boxes, one by one the old man gave in to him. When nobody was looking, Raven opened the boxes, and the precious objects inside flew out through the smoke hole and up into the dark sky.

But there was still no light in the world. Raven turned himself back into his bird form again, and took the final box, the one they call the Box of Daylight. He flew back to the river where he opened the box, and broke daylight over the Fishermen. They became frightened, and they ran away and hid. They became the creatures of the night.

But the rest of the human beings looked around and they saw their world clearly for the first time. And they marveled.

One of the many versions of The Box of Daylight legend as told by the Naa Kahidi Theater.

RIGHT: The Naa Kahidi Theater dramatizes Native legends with the use of replicas of traditional ceremonial regalia such as carved masks and Chilkat robes.
(PHOTO BY MARK KELLEY)

THREE

KLUUNAHL

THE HAIDA

When I listened to the old people talk—we ought to do this and we ought to do that—I decided to do something about it. So I invited the people: here is this time to give names to your children and to your grandchildren. Some of them flatly refused: "No, we've got to forget the old ways and move on, we are not going to do this." But those two nights they were lining up to name their children.

— Robert Davidson
Haida
Eagle

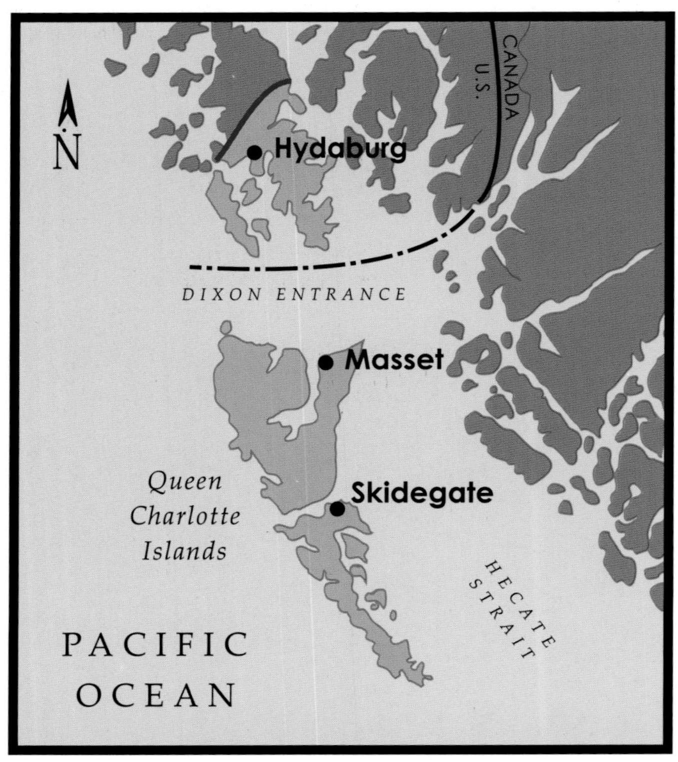

ABOVE: The Queen Charlotte Islands off the coast of northern British Columbia, known as Haida Gwaii to the Haida, are the homeland of the Haida people. The southern portion of the Alexander Archipelago in Southeast Alaska was also the territory of the Kaigani Haida, who migrated north from the Queen Charlotte Islands. Most Haida today still live on the Northwest Coast in Southeast Alaska, British Columbia, and Washington state.

(See Map on pages 14–15 for an expanded view of Alaska and the Northwest Coast.)

PAGES 50-51: The red cedar mask that Haida artist Robert Davidson calls "Dawning of the Eagle" is a self-portrait. The mask's open, clear-eyed expression symbolizes the hope he has for the future of Haida culture. The seemingly simple execution of design is deceptive, for simplicity is the hallmark of a master artist. The face is ornamented with flicker feathers, red cedar bark, and human hair. *(COURTESY ROBERT DAVIDSON)*

A RENEWAL OF PRIDE

When Haida artist Robert Davidson extended an invitation to his family and friends to attend the first potlatch held in a Haida community in recent memory, the idea was met with resistance by some. Many people had adopted western ways to the exclusion of their own cultural traditions, and there were those among them who questioned the value of embracing old traditions. But the large turnout at Davidson's potlatch was a sign of the changes to come—a rediscovering of and new appreciation for the Haida culture by older and younger generations alike.

In historical times, it was a popular misconception among non-Natives that the potlatch was a form of "war" whereby a chief gave away all his property to prompt reciprocation from a rival. Although the giving of gifts was, and is, an integral part of a potlatch, it was not done out of rivalry, but rather as a way to repay the guests who had come to participate in and witness the occasion. The word *potlatch* is Chinook jargon for the similar-sounding Nootkan word for "giving." Today, the preferred term among many Haida is *doing.*

For a society that relied on oral tradition to preserve its history, the potlatch provided a means by which the people could gather to conduct community business. The entire village would witness the proceedings, which included adoptions, the giving of ancestral names to children, marriages, funerals, house raising, and the transfer of crests, land, and other property. The business was followed by feasting, dancing, and gift giving.

By resuming the ancient tradition of potlatching, contemporary Haida have reaffirmed their links with the past. The historical center of Haida culture is the Queen Charlotte Islands, also called Haida Gwaii. The Haida and their ancestors have inhabited these foggy islands off the coast of northern British Columbia for at least six thousand years. The Queen Charlottes include two large islands and nearly 150 smaller islands that dot the waterways of the Inside Passage.

LEFT: Ravenstail weaving, so called for the resemblance of its herringbone patterns to the tail feathers of a raven, is once again becoming a familiar sight on the Northwest Coast. The skill and length of time required to weave a ravenstail robe contribute to its great value. *(ALASKA STATE MUSEUM, JUNEAU)*

The Haida were once recognized as four distinct groups: the Kaigani Haida, Northern Haida, Central Haida, and Southern Haida. The Haida's migration to what is now present-day Alaska began in the eighteenth century. They traveled across Dixon Entrance from the Queen Charlotte Islands to the southern part of the Alexander Archipelago and occupied village sites that had formerly belonged to the Tlingit. One of these villages was called Kaigani, and the name subsequently came to refer to all the Alaskan Haida.

The Haida people continue to live today on the Queen Charlotte Islands, concentrated mainly in the towns of Masset and Skidegate, both of which are historical village sites. Many Haida also live in the communities of Southeast Alaska, such as Hydaburg, Ketchikan, Craig, and Juneau. Still others live further south in Seattle, Washington, where there is a large Haida population.

Despite the geographical distance that separates them, contemporary Haida continue to share a common interest in the progress of their people.

RIGHT: Juneau artist Scott Douglas creates all his designs, including this Haida-style bracelet depicting a split raven, using traditional hand tools. A non-Native, Douglas was adopted by the Haida Double-Finned Killer Whale clan and by the Tlingit Kiks.ádi (Frog-Raven) clan of Wrangell.
(PHOTO BY TREVOR ROEHL)

BELOW: In Juneau, weavers work on one of the first ravenstail robes to be created in the last 175 years. Named "Hands Across Time," the robe's patterns represent the heritage of the weavers—Tlingit, Haida, Tsimshian, and non-Native.
(ALASKA STATE MUSEUM, JUNEAU)

This quest for self-determination has led to a cultural renewal that, in its most tangible form, can be seen in the revival of the artistic tradition. Haida artists are renowned for their skill and for their mastery of a variety of techniques. Many of these artists are passing on their knowledge to successive generations. Bill Reid, who revived the ancient art of canoe making, established training programs for apprentices in the villages of Masset and Skidegate.

In Juneau, Haida weavers have joined Tlingit, Tsimshian, and non-Native weavers to create new regalia in the ravenstail tradition, which has not been practiced since the early 1800s. This complex form of weaving takes its name from the resemblance of its herringbone patterns to the tail feathers of a raven. Ravenstail has characteristic geometric patterns, as opposed to the curvilinear representations of clan crests seen in Chilkat-style weaving, which was developed later. Ravenstail regalia, including robes, leggings, pouches, and hats, is meant to be worn. The revival of the ravenstail tradition has led to the wearing of regalia at ceremonies and gatherings, where many people are seeing ravenstail for the first time.

The resurgence of interest in cultural traditions has crossed generation lines. Young people have enthusiastically taken up dancing and singing and have been performing at *doings* and at the biennial Celebration of Native culture held in Juneau. In the classrooms, the same elders who as children were forbidden to speak their Native language in school now teach the Haida language and culture to a new generation of eager students.

ABOVE: At a potlatch given by his brother, Robert, in 1981, Reggie Davidson performs his rendition of the Eagle Dance. In Haida culture, dancing is regarded as an integral part of a happy life. The eagle headdress Davidson wears is his own creation, carved with the knowledge he gained while learning to dance. (PHOTO BY ULLI STELTZER)

There are no old male dancers in Masset anymore; it's just women who are left. So when I started to dance I had to make it up, just try to imitate the animals I was portraying. At first they didn't tell me much more than what I was doing wrong. There was Nonnie and a couple of older people sitting around when we had dance practice. "You just don't dance like women do with their hands on their hips; men don't have their hands on their hips." That's what they said, and they bawled me out. Later, when we danced and we were doing it right—I guess it took them a while to remember—they said, "That's how it is, you do it that way!"

— *Reggie Davidson*
Haida
Eagle

For the younger generation, the chance to learn firsthand from the elders has given them a sense of pride and respect for their heritage. Vicki Soboleff, a mother and artist who herself only began in the last ten years to fully appreciate her heritage, believes that "Native children in particular need to know about their culture in order to feel complete." Her sentiment reflects the growing belief among Native people of the importance of maintaining the old traditions and embracing one's heritage with pride.

The Raven Steals the Salmon from the Beaver House

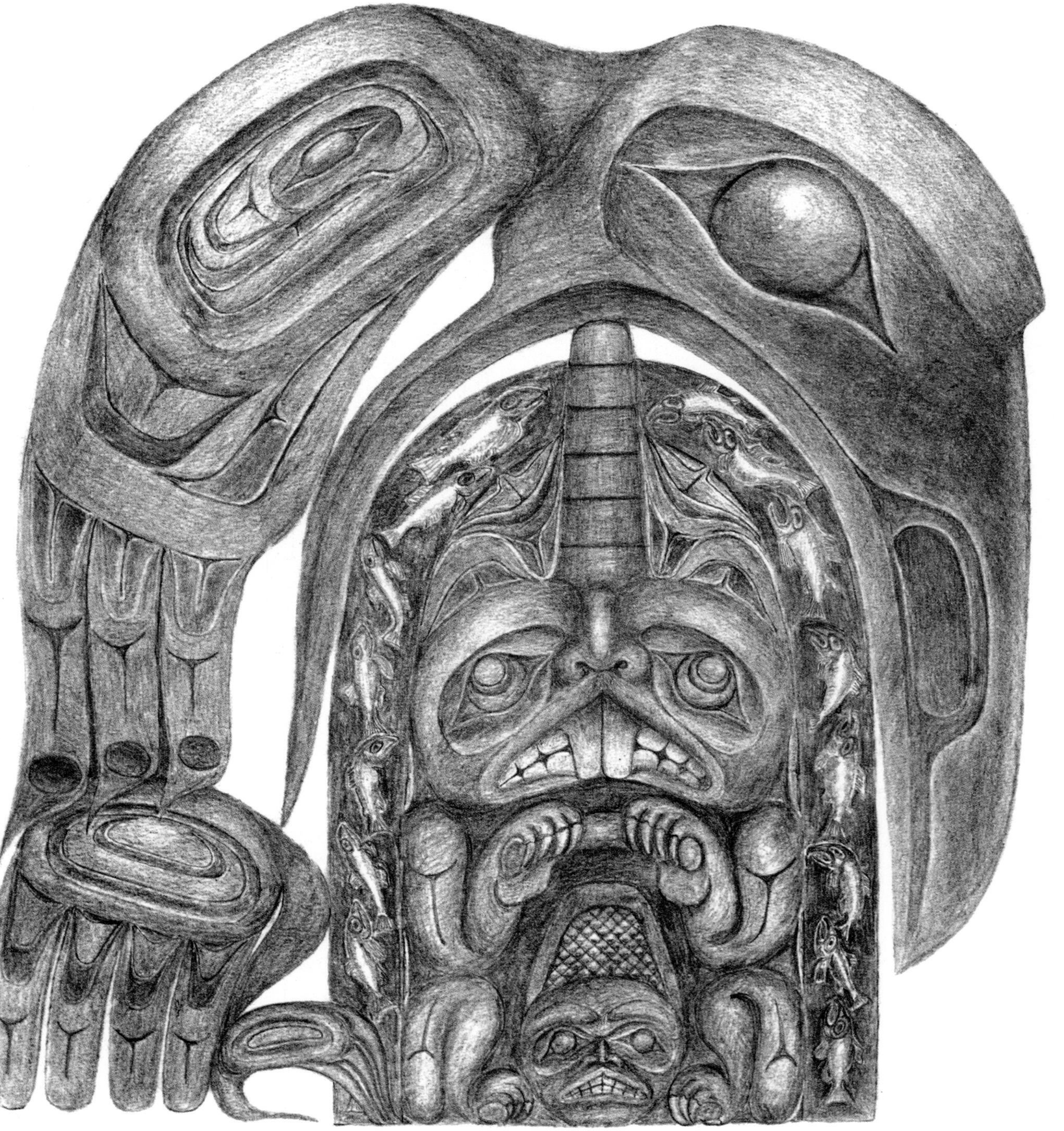

Illustration by Bill Reid ◆ Story by Bill Reid & Robert Bringhurst

(ILLUSTRATION COURTESY OF BUSCHLEN • MOWATT GALLERY, VANCOUVER, BILL REID'S EXCLUSIVE WORLDWIDE AGENT)

The Raven had grown tired of Haida Gwai and had flown to the mainland, where he had heard there were lakes and streams—things not then to be found in the Islands. The lakes and streams as such didn't interest him very much, but the thought of the tasty fish he might find in them certainly did.

He landed on a beach and was walking along feeling hungry and alone when, coming around a low headland, he met two men whom he knew to be beavers. They were very friendly, and they saw at once that the Raven was in great need of something to eat and a warm place to rest his wings. They fed him the little they had with them—and it was real food, not alder bark, such as beavers eat most of the time. No ordinary human beings such as we know them now were yet to be found on the earth. The Raven hadn't got round to creating them. But the two beavers, since they had decided to visit the beach, were in the midst of a human transformation, and so, to the Raven's delight, they not only looked like humans but were eating a rich and varied diet, just as humans like to do.

They invited him to come to their house, and the Raven gladly consented. The house wasn't far away, and when they arrived the Raven saw it was a great place indeed, a great beam-and-plank edifice with a magnificent pole in front of it. As they entered, the Raven saw a wonderfully painted screen which stretched across the rear of the house, and he seemed to hear the rush of powerful rivers and the tinkle of pleasant streams from behind the screen. Most exciting of all, he seemed to hear a sound which could only be that of a good-sized fish jumping.

The Raven asked about the sounds, as he could not recall having seen any bodies of water around the house before he came in. But the men, who were really beavers, said they could hear nothing.

One of them soon started a fire in the firepit in the center of the house. The other stepped through an opening in the screen, which shimmered most strangely in the firelight, and he came back shortly carrying two spring salmon. The two men cooked these on the fire and offered a portion to the Raven. All three had a satisfying meal and then went to sleep.

Next morning the same thing happened—one man lighting the fire, the other getting the fish from behind the screen, and all three eating until they could eat no more.

The Raven stayed in the beavers' house for many days, enjoying the food and also the company of his hosts. But one morning he woke to find that the men, who he'd known all along were beavers, had reassumed their beaver shape. Instead of the pleasant sounds of his companions preparing the morning meal, he heard only the grunts and heaves of the beavers as they cut down trees and hauled them to the lodge. And much worse, instead of succulent salmon, he was served a stick of very tough wood for his breakfast. The Raven grew suddenly homesick for his native islands and decided it was time to return.

But he certainly wasn't going home without trying to find the secret that lay behind the screen, so as soon as the beavers went out again on a tree-cutting expedition, the Raven went to the rear of the house and looked everywhere for the opening. He had no success until he remembered how one of the beavers had built up the fire before the other had penetrated the screen. He too built a fire, and when he had done that the screen seemed to dissolve like coastal mist before him. He walked right through the insubstantial images which had been solid wood before, and found himself looking out over a vast expanse of land dotted and traced with lakes and rivers, all of them full of fish and all of the fish making their way to their home waters to spawn and die.

The Raven in his excitement tried to pick up as many fish as possible to take home with him, but trying as he did to hold so many at a time, he kept on dropping all of them.

He sat down and thought about what he could do. "It's nice country," he said, "but it's sort of flat, not like the Islands. I wonder what would happen if I lifted the corner of it here and tried to roll it into something I could handle." So the Raven pulled at the ground near his feet, and he found it came loose from the bedrock quite easily. He started rolling it up like a cedarbark blanket, and after a short time he had all the lakes and rivers and streams in a neat, convenient roll, which he took in his strong beak. Then he flew rapidly back through the screen and headed for the Islands.

Before he arrived, a lot of the water from the rolled-up rivers had drained away, but many of the streams and the little lakes remained. And most importantly, the fish were safe.

When he reached the Islands at last, the Raven was tired from carrying his load, and he was happy to drop the roll and let what remained of the lakes and streams fall where they might. That's why today nearly every one of the Haida Islands is spattered with little lakes and small but very rich streams—the refuge each year for millions of spawning salmon, some of which still provide welcome meals for the Raven and all his relations.

FOUR

TXAAP

THE TSIMSHIAN

Artists from long ago inspire new generations of Indians to carry on the traditions of which they began. I am determined and dedicated to become the finest artist that I can be while at the same time helping to revitalize and carry on the rich culture of my tribe. I want my sons and other young Indian people to be proud of their heritage.

—David Boxley
Alaskan Tsimshian
Lax-skeek (Eagle Clan)

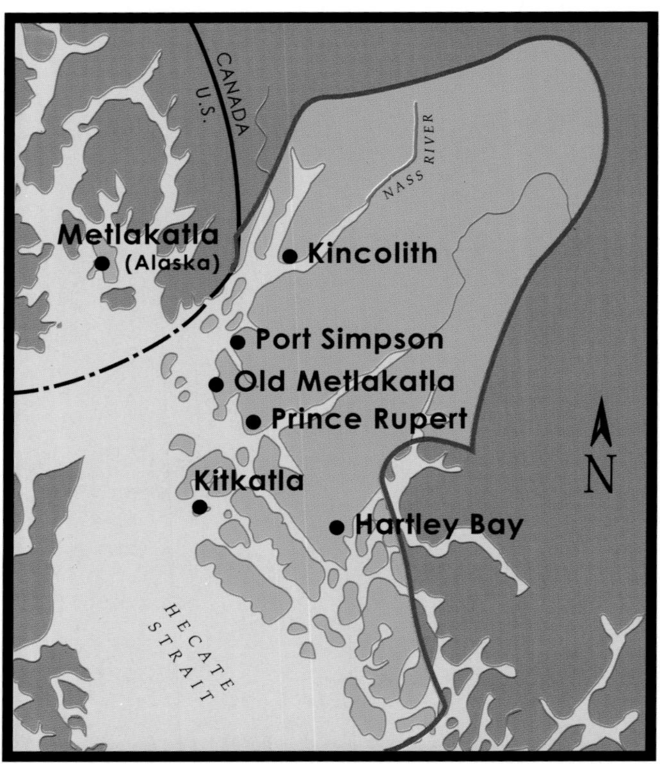

ABOVE: The Tsimshian historically lived along the coast and in the interior of northern British Columbia. In 1887, a group of Tsimshian moved to Alaska from British Columbia and established the community of New Metlakatla on Annette Island. Today, many Tsimshian continue to live in (New) Metlakatla as well as in other cities and small towns throughout Southeast Alaska and British Columbia.

(See Map on pages 14–15 for an expanded view of Alaska and the Northwest Coast.)

PAGES 58–59: Carved screens were traditionally used to partition off a section of the communal house. This detail from a contemporary screen by artist and carving instructor Jack Hudson depicts an eagle with spread wings. The figures on the screen were inspired by a Tsimshian myth that relates how the Eagle Clan obtained the beaver crest.

(PHOTO BY STEVEN SHRUM)

INSPIRATION FOR THE FUTURE

The observance of the 100th anniversary of the Alaskan community of Metlakatla in 1987 was no ordinary event. For Metlakatla's Tsimshian residents, it was a time to celebrate—a time to express pride in their cultural heritage. In the last twenty years, Metlakatla has become a center for the revival of Tsimshian culture. Through the work of many dedicated people, age-old traditions are being preserved and passed on to a new generation.

The determination and spirit of cooperation that exist in Metlakatla have their roots in the community's origin. Under the lead of an Anglican missionary named William Duncan who had worked for twenty-five years to establish a community of over a thousand believers in Metlakatla, British Columbia, a group of Tsimshian moved north from British Columbia in 1887 to found New Metlakatla, Alaska. The society they created was utopian by design. A belief in the common good, rather than individual profit, fostered a strong sense of community that persists in Metlakatla to this day.

Metlakatla has had a colorful and often turbulent history, owing largely to the competition between religious factions that divided the community at the end of the nineteenth century. For years, Duncan and his supporters clashed with Presbyterian minister Edward Marsden. Marsden, a Tsimshian, advocated the establishment of a Native chiefdom to replace the existing government. Although Marsden was unsuccessful, the dissension resulted in the formation of a city council type of government whereby the Tsimshian people elected traditional tribal leaders to office.

Given its unique history and the fact that it is the only predominantly Tsimshian community in the state, Metlakatla is distinct from other Alaska Native communities. Many of its residents trace their lineages to ancestors who lived along the coast and the inland rivers of present-day British Columbia. Today, most Tsimshian continue to live in

ABOVE: The Git Lax Liksht'aa Dance Group of Metlakatla was founded to give young people the opportunity to learn traditional Tsimshian dances. Participation in the group has given the children a renewed sense of pride in their heritage.
(COURTESY ANNETTE ISLAND SCHOOL DISTRICT)

British Columbia in communities such as Port Simpson, Prince Rupert, and Hartley Bay, as well as other areas on the Northwest Coast. The Tsimshianic-speaking communities are recognized as four separate groups based on language: the Coast and Southern Tsimshian, Nisga'a, and Gitksan.

Unlike their ancestors who were encouraged to abandon their cultural traditions, the Tsimshian residents of Metlakatla take pride in their heritage and have developed a renewed interest in their Native culture. The quest to learn more about traditional ways has sparked a contemporary revival of Native song, dance, and art. Visits to their community by Tsimshian people from British Columbia, where language and cultural practices were somewhat less disrupted, have been a welcome part of the renewal.

The legacy of Metlakatla's past is the cooperative nature and the desire of dedicated individuals to share their time and knowledge with others. One such person is artist and teacher Jack Hudson. As a Tsimshian who was raised with little knowledge of his people's traditions, he recognizes the importance of having a cultural identity. Today, Hudson is renowned throughout the world as a master carver, but it was not always so. Unlike his students, he had no one to teach him how to create Native wood carvings using traditional methods. He learned the hard way—by reading everything

he could, through studying existing works, and by talking to old artists.

Before Hudson's students take tool to wood, he teaches them to recognize the animals of the Northwest Coast. The animals, along with characters from Tsimshian legends, provide the inspiration for artistic designs. After mastering the drawing of animals by freehand, the students learn to paint. But it is not until the students have fashioned their own tools—Native tools are not manufactured commercially—that they begin to carve their first piece.

The dedication shown by Hudson and his students in learning Tsimshian traditions is not unique to them. The establishment of the Native Education Programs in Metlakatla has given other elders in the community the opportunity to pass on their knowledge and skills to the children. Through the programs, children are taught the Tsimshian language, dance, art, and the traditions of their people. Elaine Guthrie, one of the founders and teachers of the Git Lax Liksht'aa Dance Group, believes that by learning the traditions, children become proud of who they are.

For Guthrie, the necessity of preserving the Tsimshian culture cannot be understated. "We grew up in primarily a white culture," she recalls. "Carving, dancing, and our Tsimshian language were something we knew nothing about. Now we are slowly trying to get back what we almost lost." With the belief that there is no activity more important than working with the children of their community, Guthrie and other dedicated teachers like her are giving a new generation a direction for the future.

LEFT: This thirty-five-foot totem pole by Tsimshian artist David Boxley was commissioned by a S'Klallam (Coast Salish) leader from Port Gamble, Washington. From the top, the pole shows a thunderbird, a S'Klallam man holding onto the tail of a killer whale, a grizzly bear, and a raven. The pole is carved in the Alaskan Tsimshian style, but its owner requested the artist to include the outspread wings of the thunderbird in the style of the southern Northwest Coast tradition. *(PHOTO BY DAVID BOXLEY)*

ABOVE: A verse in the Book of Revelation was the inspiration for this carving by Tsimshian artist Roxana Leask. The carved wooden screen shows a woman with child kneeling on a moon box. The screen is carved from red cedar and decorated with abalone inlay. *(COURTESY ROXANA LEASK)*

BELOW: There has been renewed effort in recent years to teach children the value of their cultural traditions. At annual culture camps, young people learn traditional methods for obtaining and preparing food. *(COURTESY CHILKOOT CULTURE CAMP)*